BRITAIN'S RAILWAY HOTELS

MICHAEL PATTERSON

AMBERLEY

Glorious revival – the former Midland Grand, now the St Pancras Renaissance Hotel, London. (Steve Poole, 2011)

Map illustration on p.6 by Thomas Bohon, User Design, Illustration and Typesetting.

First published 2016

Amberley Publishing
The Hill, Stroud
Gloucestershire, GL5 4EP

www.amberley-books.com

Copyright © Michael Patterson, 2016

The right of Michael Patterson to be identified
as the Author of this work has been asserted in
accordance with the Copyrights, Designs and
Patents Act 1988.

ISBN 978 1 4456 5434 8 (print)
ISBN 978 1 4456 5435 5 (ebook)

British Library Cataloguing in Publication Data.
A catalogue record for this book is available from
the British Library.

Typesetting by Amberley Publishing.
Printed in the UK.

Introduction

The opening of the Grand Junction Railway from Birmingham to Lancashire in 1837 and completion of the London & Birmingham Railway in 1838 made it possible for the first time to travel by train between London, Birmingham, Liverpool and Manchester. The railways began to take on the appearance of a national network rather than a collection of unconnected lines serving local needs, but trains were slow, uncomfortable and lacked even basic facilities. Long journeys could take more than a day while poor connections and infrequent services could leave passengers stranded. Making a return journey in a single day – something we now take for granted – was a realistic prospect only for relatively short trips.

The coming of the railways created an upsurge in demand for hotel accommodation and the railway companies soon realised that this could be profitable business. The London & Birmingham Railway opened the first two railway-owned hotels at London's Euston terminus in 1839, but the company had to improvise to meet demand at Birmingham by hurriedly converting the top floor of the station building at Curzon Street into a small hotel.

By the early 1840s the rail network was growing rapidly. Hotels were built at key junction stations such as Derby, Swindon and Normanton (Yorkshire) where important routes converged. During the same decade, lines began to reach the coastal ports, enabling the railways to connect with shipping services to Europe, Ireland or parts of Britain still inaccessible by rail. A railway hotel was built at Fleetwood, from where passengers for the west of Scotland had to complete their journey by sea, and at Newhaven and Folkestone where the railway companies started their own cross-Channel shipping services.

The first great railway hotels in London and the big cities appeared in the 1850s but the real building boom came between 1860 and 1900. By the turn of the century all the London hotels and most of those in the towns and cities of Britain had been built, a final flourish in the early years of the twentieth century seeing the opening of some of the grandest of the big city hotels in Edinburgh, Manchester and Liverpool.

It was not long before the railway companies started exploiting the growing demand for holiday accommodation. This began in the 1860s with hotels at seaside resorts

Edinburgh Castle as backdrop – The Caledonian, now the Waldorf Astoria, Edinburgh. (Waldorf Astoria Hotels & Resorts, 2014)

and tourist hotels in areas like the Lake District. In 1899 the Great North of Scotland Railway built a hotel at Cruden Bay on the Aberdeenshire coast specifically aimed at attracting golfers. Other golfing hotels followed in the early years of the twentieth century, although perhaps the greatest of all, at Gleneagles, was delayed by the First World War.

By the time Gleneagles opened in 1924 the alphabet soup of pre-war railways had been amalgamated into just four companies through the 1923 Grouping – the London & North Eastern (LNER), London Midland & Scottish (LMS), Southern (SR), and Great Western (GWR). The Big Four went on to consolidate the hotels under their control into some of the most successful hotel groups in the country.

In all, the railway companies built, bought or leased well over 100 hotels, seventy-five of which feature in this book. A veritable who's who of the leading British architects of the day were commissioned to design them, including Philip Hardwick, Lewis Cubitt, Edward Middleton Barry, Francis Thompson, Alfred Waterhouse, Decimus Burton and Sir George Gilbert Scott.

Not all the railway hotels survived. Indeed, some had very short lives. Even the mighty Midland Grand at St Pancras succumbed; its outdated facilities and the army of people needed to keep it running made it unprofitable by the time it closed in 1935.

In the Second World War the railway hotels played a significant role. Many were requisitioned for use as hospitals or to provide accommodation for military personnel. Some became military installations, such as the South Western Hotel at Southampton, which became HMS *Shrapnel*. It was here that General Eisenhower briefed Winston

Churchill on the preparations for D-Day. The Fishguard Bay Hotel became a secret base for testing submersibles. The Deepdene Hotel near Dorking and its underground tunnels became the Southern Railway's wartime operational headquarters, from where the transport of 320,000 men evacuated from Dunkirk in May–June 1940 was controlled.

By the end of the war some of the hotels were in a poor state, including several that had suffered serious bomb damage. The railways themselves were worn out after six years of war and the government nationalised them and their hotels in 1948. With the need for vast amounts of investment to repair and modernise the railways, more than a dozen of the hotels were sold off as a way of raising money between 1948 and 1953. The remaining hotels then came under the control of British Transport Hotel and Catering Services and, in 1963, British Transport Hotels Ltd (BTH), a subsidiary of the British Railways Board.

By the 1980s the BTH hotels were suffering from a prolonged lack of investment and many were looking shabby and in need of modernisation. There was no way that a cash-strapped nationalised industry like the railways was ever going to find the money to bring them up to modern standards and, in 1982–84, the BTH portfolio was sold off. Thirty years on, most of them have benefited from major investment, creating some of the most prestigious hotels in the land. Even one or two of the hotels closed in earlier times have reopened, most notably at St Pancras where the Renaissance Hotel has restored the glory that was once the Midland Grand.

I hope this book will help the reader to share my admiration for the fascinating history and grand architecture of the railway hotels, the vaulting ambition that led to their construction, and their dedication to serving their guests – in some cases for more than 150 years.

Dornoch

Strathpeffer

Inverness

Cruden Bay

Kyle of Lochalsh

Aberdeen

Perth

Gleneagles

St. Andrews

Edinburgh

Glasgow

Ayr

Turnberry

Dumfries

Newcastle

Hartlepool

Keswick

Saltburn

Morecambe

York

Fleetwood

Bradford

Preston

Leeds

Hull

Manchester

Normanton

Grimsby

Holyhead

Liverpool

Crewe

Sheffield

Blaenau Ffestiniog

Stoke

Derby

Birmingham

Peterborough

Stratford-upon-Avon

Fishguard

Parkeston Quay

Felixstowe

Neyland

Harwich

Swindon

LONDON

Port Victoria

Dorking

Dover

Southampton

Hythe

Folkestone

Newhaven

Moretonhampstead

St Ives

0   50   100 km

Index of hotel locations

Junction Hotels

As the railway network developed, lines converged at what became key junction stations, where passengers could make connections or transfer between different operators. Some of the earliest railway hotels were built at these locations.

Normanton station and station hotel, Yorkshire, 1986. (Keith Long)

In the early days of railways, dining cars and on-train refreshments were still things yet to come. Instead, long-distance expresses were timetabled to make extended stops at important junctions such as Normanton to allow passengers to obtain food and drink from the refreshment room. Hot food was prepared in the station hotel, built in 1840, and carried over the footbridge to the refreshment room on the platforms. With a trainload of passengers all wanting to be served at once, it must have been quite a crush. The Midland Railway bought the hotel in 1861. It closed for residential purposes in 1902 and was demolished in the late 1980s.

Crewe Arms Hotel, Crewe, Cheshire, 2015. (Malcolm Rhead)

In 1837, the tiny hamlet of Crewe was transformed by the arrival of the Grand Junction Railway. A year earlier local landowner Lord Crewe began construction of the Tudor-style Crewe Arms Hotel next to what would become one of Britain's busiest junction stations. The London & North Western Railway leased the hotel in 1864, bought it outright in 1877 and extended it in 1880 when the date was added to the Crewe family's coat-of-arms on the central gable. In 1923 it became an LMS hotel. It was sold in 1952 following nationalisation. It is now a Best Western hotel and can claim to be one of the oldest railway hotels in the world.

Crewe family's coat-of-arms on the centre gable, 2010. (Failing Angel)

Midland Hotel, Derby, 2008. (Hugh Llewelyn)

Built in 1837–41, Derby station and the Midland Hotel were among the pioneering developments of the railway age. Designed by Francis Thompson, a leading architect of the era, the red-brick Georgian-style hotel is H-shaped, with two parallel blocks linked together. Besides rail users, it catered for tourists visiting the nearby Derbyshire Dales. The hotel operated independently until the Midland Railway bought it in 1862. In 1923 it became an LMS hotel and, after nationalisation, a British Transport Hotel. Sold in 1982, it is now a Hallmark Hotel, making it one of the railway hotels with the longest continuous service.

Midland Hotel showing the parallel blocks, 2008. (Tom Bastin)

Queens Royal Hotel, Swindon station. (John Law Collection)

The GWR's station at Swindon opened in 1842. Twin blocks on the two main platforms included refreshment rooms at platform level and hotel accommodation on the first floor. The covered footbridge over the tracks connected the bedrooms in one block with the sitting rooms and coffee room in the other. The hotel started out as the Queens Arms Inn in 1842 and was later renamed the Queens Royal Hotel. It closed in 1898.

Great Northern Hotel, Peterborough, 2016. (Author)

The Great Northern Railway's hotel at Peterborough opened in 1851. An immediate success, the Great Northern Hotel was extended in 1856. It became an LNER hotel in 1923 and later a British Transport Hotel, when it was again extended, this time in a modern style. Sold in 1983, it remains open.

North Stafford Hotel, Stoke-on-Trent, c. 1900. (Author's collection)

Opened in 1849, the North Staffordshire Railway's hotel stands on an attractive square opposite the station. The Jacobean-style brick façade of the North Stafford Hotel is characterised by Dutch gables and tall chimneys. E-shaped, in the style of an Elizabethan manor house, it was enlarged in 1878. In 1923 it became an LMS hotel. It had long been leased out and an inspection in 1931 found it in poor condition. The hotel was promptly closed, modernised and reopened in 1933, this time operated by the LMS itself. Following nationalisation it was sold in 1953. It remains open as an eighty-bedroom Britannia Hotel. The building is listed Grade II*.

The North Stafford in 2014. (Mark Wheaver)

Royal York Hotel, 2014. (J. L. Berghout)

The North Eastern Railway's first station hotel at York opened in 1853. Queen Victoria visited in 1854, hence the title 'Royal'. In 1878 William Peachey's much larger 100-bedroom hotel next to the new station replaced it. Built in yellow brick in a vaguely Italian Gothic style, it was enlarged in 1896 by the addition of a new wing. The public rooms are impressive in scale and give fine views of York Minster. In 1923 the Royal Station Hotel was transferred to the LNER and, after nationalisation, joined the BTH group. An annexe, the Friars Garden Hotel, was added in 1981. Sold in 1983 and renamed the Royal York Hotel, it is now part of the PH Hotels group.

Royal Station Hotel, York, *c.* 1915 – lounge complete with red pillar box. (Author's collection)

Royal Highland Hotel, Inverness, Scotland, 2015. (Peter Koppers)

The station hotel at Inverness was designed in 1855 by Joseph Mitchell, who engineered much of the Highland Railway. Its most prominent external feature is a tower above the entrance. Internally, fixtures and fittings are typical of the quality craftsmanship found in railway hotels of the period. The ornate T-shaped staircase is said to have been the model for the grand staircase of the liner *Titanic*, while the dining room retains its elegant proportions and decorative detailing. The Highland Railway bought the hotel in 1878. Transferred to the LMS in 1923, it later became a BTH hotel. It was sold in 1983 and now welcomes guests as the Royal Highland Hotel.

Dining room, 2015. (Peter Koppers)

Station hotel, Dumfries, Scotland, 1890s. (Library of Congress*)

When the station hotel first opened in 1865, Dumfries was a key railway junction in south-west Scotland. The hotel was bought by the Glasgow & South Western Railway around 1880. Built of sandstone with a distinctive roof featuring dormers and a cupola, the hotel was rebuilt in 1897 with twenty-nine bedrooms. In 1923 it became an LMS hotel and later a British Transport Hotel. Sold in 1972, it is now a Best Western hotel.

Station hotel, Perth, Scotland, 2011. (Mike Brocklebank)

Perth's station hotel opened in 1865, jointly owned by the Caledonian, North British and Highland railways. In 1890 it was rebuilt in Scottish Baronial style with gables and a tower. A covered passageway from the station encouraged Queen Victoria to use the hotel on train journeys to Balmoral. In 1923 it became an LMS hotel and, after nationalisation, a British Transport Hotel. Sold in 1983, the seventy-bedroom hotel remains open.

Park Hotel, Preston, Lancashire. (Mike Craig, 2012)

The Park Hotel opened in 1882 as a joint venture by the Lancashire & Yorkshire and London & North Western railways. The vast red-brick pile, with its gables, turrets, outsize chimneys and distinctive tower, was connected to Preston station by a covered footbridge. From its hilltop location, the hotel overlooked the station on one side and Miller Park and the River Ribble on the other. Intended as a stopping-off point on long Anglo-Scottish journeys, the introduction of faster trains meant that its fortunes started declining early in the twentieth century. Acquired by the LMS in 1923, the Park was sold in 1950 and converted for use as council offices.

Rear view of the hotel, now council offices, 2015. (Author)

Port Hotels

As the network expanded, the railway companies were keen to link up with coastal shipping services as well as those to Europe, Ireland and the Americas. The uncertainties and discomfort associated with sea crossings and long-distance train travel in the Victorian era made the ports obvious places to build hotels for passengers transferring between train and ship.

North Euston Hotel, Fleetwood, Lancashire, 2007. (Alistair Parker)

In the early 1840s there was no railway through the Lake District, and so passengers from London for the west of Scotland had to travel by train to Fleetwood and continue their journey by sea. The Preston & Wyre Railway opened a hotel in the town and, as passengers had started out from Euston, named it the North Euston Hotel. The architect Decimus Burton designed a semi-circular hotel, giving every room a sea view. It opened in 1841, but by the 1850s the railway to Scotland had been completed. The hotel closed in 1859 and was sold to the War Office. The town later prospered as a seaside resort so the North Euston reopened in 1899. It remains open today.

ROYAL PAVILION HOTEL, FOLKESTONE.

Royal Pavilion Hotel, Folkestone, Kent. (Author's collection)

The thirty-five-bedroom Royal Pavilion Hotel was opened by the South Eastern Railway in 1843, primarily to serve passengers using its shipping services. With faster journey times by both rail and ship, the need for overnight accommodation gradually declined. The SER sold the hotel in 1896, after which it was greatly expanded. A small part of the hotel was incorporated into the Grand Burstin Hotel, which opened in 1984.

London & Paris Hotel, Newhaven, Sussex, *c.* 1910. ('Our Newhaven' collection)

The London Brighton & South Coast Railway reached Newhaven in 1847 and began operating steamer services to Dieppe. The company built the London & Paris Hotel to accommodate passengers who were stranded because of strong winds or the silting of the creek. Transferred to the Southern Railway in 1923, the hotel served as HMS *Aggressive* during the Second World War. It was bombed in 1942 and demolished in the 1950s.

South Wales Hotel, Neyland, Wales, 1890s. (Library of Congress*)

The South Wales Hotel was opened in 1858 by the South Wales Railway, which was absorbed by the GWR in 1863. The twelve bedrooms were increased to twenty when Neyland briefly attracted transatlantic shipping services in the 1860s. Subsequently the hotel relied mainly on passengers using shipping services to Ireland, but in 1906 even this trade was lost to Fishguard. The GWR sold the hotel in 1922. It was demolished in 1972.

Station Hotel, Holyhead, Wales, *c.* 1906. (Author's collection)

In 1880 the London & North Western Railway rebuilt Holyhead station and replaced the small Royal Hotel with the larger Station Hotel. Located at the harbour, the four-storey, red-brick hotel was ideally placed for passengers using shipping services to Ireland. In 1923 ownership transferred to the LMS. It closed in 1951 and was demolished in 1978.

Royal Station Hotel, Hull, in NER days. (Author's collection)

Designed by G. T. Andrews, the York & North Midland Railway's station hotel opened in 1851. The symmetrical Italianate three-storey façade featured arcades and a balustraded portico, flanked by two slightly projecting wings. Built in the form of a hollow square, the enclosed central courtyard housed the reception area and lounge, which were surrounded by an arcade leading to the large public rooms. Advertising itself as a commercial and family hotel, the 120 rooms included coffee lounges, a billiard room and numerous suites.

The arcaded façade, which has lost the original portico. (Mercure Hull Royal Hotel)

Hull Royal Hotel – the arcaded lounge. (Mercure Hull Royal Hotel)

Patrons included passengers using the shipping routes from Hull to Scandinavia and Northern Europe. In 1854 the new North Eastern Railway took over and changed the name to Royal Station Hotel to mark a visit from Queen Victoria the previous year. Absorbed by the LNER in 1923, it was extended in 1931/2 to provide additional accommodation and an art deco entrance from the station. After nationalisation the hotel was a British Transport Hotel until 1983. The interior was badly damaged by fire in 1990 but the hotel was restored and reopened in 1992. It is now the Mercure Hull Royal Hotel. The building is listed Grade II*.

Art deco entrance from the station, 2013. (Bernard Sharp)

Lord Warden Hotel, Dover, Kent, *c.* 1920. (Author's collection)

Victorian travellers took it for granted that a journey to the Continent would be lengthy and unpredictable, and so would often take it in stages. In 1853 the South Eastern Railway opened the eighty-bedroom Lord Warden Hotel, designed in Italianate style by Samuel Beazley. A covered walkway from the first floor provided direct access to Dover Town station. In 1855 Emperor Napoleon III of France and Empress Eugenie were received at the hotel before departing for London on a state visit. In 1871, in less happy circumstances, the emperor was reunited with his wife here after being deposed following the disastrous Franco-Prussian War.

The former hotel in 2015. (Gareth Williams)

Plaque commemorating the Lord Warden's wartime role as HMS *WASP*. (Gareth Williams, 2015)

Ownership transferred to the Southern Railway in 1923 and the Lord Warden closed on the outbreak of the Second World War. From 1940–44 it became HMS *WASP*, Coastal Forces headquarters for the protection of Channel and North Sea shipping against enemy naval forces. It was sold in 1946 and converted to offices.

Port Victoria Hotel, Kent, 1905. (Medway City Archive)

The South Eastern Railway opened the line to Port Victoria in 1882. The station was located on a pier in the River Medway in the hope of attracting Continental shipping services. The company opened the single-storey weather-boarded Port Victoria Hotel in 1883 but the ships never came. Owned by the Southern Railway from 1923, the pier was declared unsafe in 1931. The hotel closed in 1949 and was demolished in 1952.

Great Eastern Hotel, Harwich, 1900. (Gavin Bleakley's collection)

The Great Eastern Railway's line to Harwich opened in 1854 and the company established a shipping service to Rotterdam in 1863. To accommodate passengers, the company opened the thirty-nine-bedroom Great Eastern Hotel alongside the harbour in 1865. The architect Thomas Allom chose an Italianate style. A large central pediment containing a clock dominates the façade, which also features roundels portraying historical figures. A first-floor balcony and a platform on the roof offered guests panoramic views over the harbour and River Orwell.

The hotel in 1912. (Gavin Bleakley's collection)

The former Great Eastern Hotel, 2012. (Simon Evans)

The hotel's opening was a grand affair, with a special train bringing VIPs from London. A dinner for 200 people, accompanied by numerous speeches and toasts, took so long that guests had to make a hasty departure to catch the special train back to London. After shipping services were removed to the new quay at nearby Parkeston in 1882/3, the Great Eastern was extensively refurbished but patronage declined. It closed temporarily from 1908–12 and for good in 1922. The building was requisitioned by the Admiralty in both world wars and became Harwich Town Hall in 1951. In 1988 the building was converted into flats.

Four of the historical figures depicted on the façade, 2012. (Simon Evans)

Former South Western Hotel, Southampton, 2010. (Jack Guilliams)

Built in 1867, the privately owned Imperial Hotel overshadowed the London & South Western Railway's Terminus station next door. Designed by John Norton, the imposing brick and stone façade is in French Renaissance style. The most prominent feature is a giant curved pediment over the main entrance, containing a roundel depicting the head of Queen Victoria. Inside, a magnificent entrance hall leads into a lounge with gilded marble walls and columns. The rapid growth of shipping services to France, the Americas and Africa brought large numbers of passengers to Southampton, prompting the LSWR to purchase the hotel in 1882.

Curved pediment with roundel depicting Queen Victoria's head, 2009. (Ian Taylor)

Former South Western Hotel – entrance hall, 2009. (Ian Taylor)

Renamed the South Western, it was from this hotel that many passengers embarked on the fateful maiden voyage of the *Titanic* in 1912. Ownership passed to the Southern Railway in 1923, but it closed on the outbreak of the Second World War and was taken over by the military, becoming HMS *Shrapnel*. Here the Supreme Allied Commander, General Eisenhower, briefed Prime Minister Winston Churchill about the D-Day landings in 1944. The hotel was sold in 1946 having already been made into offices, later occupied by the BBC. In 1998 the building was converted into flats, although the lounge and some other public rooms have been preserved.

Lounge, 2010. (Jack Guilliams)

Palace Hotel, Aberdeen. (Royan's collection)

First opened in 1874, the Palace Hotel was purchased by the Great North of Scotland Railway in 1890. It was such a success that two additional storeys were added in 1894, increasing the number of bedrooms to seventy-seven. In 1896 the hotel was able to lure guests with the prospect of salmon fishing on the River Dee after the manager secured a five-year lease. Under the ownership of the LNER from 1923, the hotel met an untimely end in October 1941 when it was destroyed by fire, the cause of which was never satisfactorily established. Six members of staff trapped in their attic rooms died in the inferno. It was not rebuilt.

Lounge. (Author's collection)

Station hotel, Aberdeen, Scotland, 2011. (Elizabeth Thomsen)

Originally opened in 1870, the fifty-one-bedroom station hotel was purchased by the Great North of Scotland Railway in 1910 following the success of the company's Palace Hotel, which was often full in summer. In 1923 the station hotel joined the LNER Hotels group and after nationalisation eventually became a British Transport Hotel. It was sold in 1983 and remains open as a Cairn Group hotel.

Lochalsh Hotel, Kyle of Lochalsh, Scotland, 2015. (Fiona MacKintosh)

When the Highland Railway's line from Dingwall reached Kyle of Lochalsh in 1897, the company bought Kyle House for conversion into a hotel. The Lochalsh Hotel is set in magnificent mountain scenery alongside the former ferry slipway, now replaced by the Skye Bridge. In 1923 it became an LMS hotel and was extensively rebuilt in 1932–35. After the Second World War it became a British Transport Hotel until 1983. It remains open.

Great Eastern Hotel, Parkeston Quay, Harwich. (Harwich & Dovercourt collection)

In 1882/3 the Great Eastern Railway built Parkeston Quay near Harwich as a new base for its shipping services to Europe. The development included a new station and the Great Eastern Hotel. In 1923 the hotel was transferred to the LNER and, following nationalisation, became a British Transport Hotel until closure in 1963, when it was converted into offices.

Grand Hotel, Hartlepool, 2015. (Brian Evans)

The North Eastern Railway's first hotel in Hartlepool was the Royal, purchased in 1880. Needing larger premises, the company acquired the Grand Hotel in 1912 and sold the Royal. The hotel was popular with passengers using ferry services to Scandinavia and Northern Europe. In 1923 the Grand became an LNER hotel and then a state-owned British Transport Hotel, which it remained until 1983. Today it is a Best Western hotel.

Yarborough Hotel, Grimsby, Lincolnshire, 2012. (David Wright)

The Manchester Sheffield & Lincolnshire Railway bought two hotels in Grimsby in 1890 – the Royal near the docks and the Yarborough by the station. The latter was originally built in 1851 and was wrecked in an infamous election riot in 1862. Before 1914 both hotels attracted passengers using the Great Central Railway's shipping services to the Continent. They became part of the LNER in 1923. After railway nationalisation, both hotels were sold off, the Royal in 1949 and the Yarborough in 1952. The Royal was demolished in 1966, the Yarborough having narrowly escaped the same fate. After many years as a pub-restaurant, work is underway to reopen the Yarborough as a thirty-nine-bedroom hotel.

Royal Hotel, Grimsby. (Author's collection)

Hotel Wyncliffe, Fishguard, Wales, 1890s. (Library of Congress*)

Believing in Fishguard's potential as a transatlantic port, the GWR bought Wyncliffe House and its extensive grounds in 1898 for conversion into a prestigious hotel. In 1906 Irish shipping services previously operating from Neyland transferred to Fishguard's new harbour, and the hotel was extended to forty bedrooms and renamed the Fishguard Bay Hotel. Ocean liners called at Fishguard from 1908, but the First World War ended the transatlantic trade. During the Second World War, the hotel was a Special Operations Executive base for testing submersibles. The hotel closed in 1950 and was sold, but later reopened and remains in use.

Fishguard Bay Hotel, 2015. (Scott Lewis)

London Hotels

After the first two railway hotels in London were opened by the London & Birmingham Railway at Euston in 1839, it was more than a decade before the other railway companies began to follow suit. By the end of the nineteenth century, ten great railway hotels had been built in the capital.

Charing Cross Hotel, *c*. 1900. (Frank Sweeney Collection)

The South Eastern Railway's 250-bedroom Charing Cross Hotel opened in 1865. It was so successful that in 1878 a large new annexe was linked to the main hotel by a footbridge. Designed by Edward Middleton Barry in French Renaissance style, the hotel shares the ground floor with the station entrance. Some public rooms survive as originally designed, two having distinctive conservatories overlooking the Strand. The ballroom has a richly ornamented ceiling. It was once the hotel restaurant, named after the former poet laureate and heritage campaigner Sir John Betjeman, who called it 'the most finely appointed dining room in London'.

Main entrance with first-floor conservatory. (Amba Hotel Charing Cross)

The façade's strong horizontal lines contrast with the tall, slim replica cross in the forecourt. Also designed by Barry, this bit of fakery marks the nearby site of an original long-lost Eleanor Cross. In 1923 the Charing Cross Hotel passed to the Southern Railway. During the Second World War the hotel suffered bomb damage and the top two floors were later rebuilt with a flat roof, leaving the skyline devoid of the turrets, dormers, chimneys and pavilions that had previously given the exterior so much character. After nationalisation, the Charing Cross became one of the flagships of the BTH group. Sold in 1983, it is now the Amba Hotel Charing Cross.

Ceiling of the ballroom, formerly the Betjeman Restaurant. (Amba Hotel Charing Cross)

Euston Hotel in LNWR days. (Author's collection)

In 1839, the London & Birmingham Railway built the twin Victoria and Euston hotels at its new London terminus. Designed by Philip Hardwick, the Euston catered primarily for First Class passengers, while accommodation at the Victoria was more basic. Having two separate hotels was not ideal, and so in 1881 the LNWR built a new block to link them, increasing the number of rooms at the combined hotel to 300. Ownership passed to the LMS in 1923 and to BTH after nationalisation. The original station, the hotel and Euston Arch were all demolished in 1961–63 to make way for the new Euston station.

Euston Hotel shortly before closure and demolition, 1962. (Ben Brooksbank)

Great Western Royal Hotel, Paddington, 1890s. (Library of Congress*)

In 1851 the Great Western Railway decided to rebuild its London terminus at Paddington. Isambard Kingdom Brunel, the driving force behind both the GWR and the development of ocean-going steamships, believed that a new grand hotel would be a suitable starting point for transatlantic journeys by train and ship from London to New York. Designed by P. C. Hardwick, the façade of the Great Western Royal Hotel is flanked by two outsize towers. A giant central pediment contains sculptures representing Peace, Plenty, Science and Industry, reflecting the self-confidence of the mid-Victorian era. Prince Albert opened the hotel in 1854.

Peace, Plenty, Science and Industry, 2015. (David Denny)

Hilton London Paddington, 2009. (Hilton Hotels & Resorts)

There were four main floors, with some of the 103 bedrooms having sitting or dressing rooms. Kitchens were in the basement and the attics were for use by guests' servants. Subsequent additions increased capacity to nearly 250 bedrooms. The hotel was extended and much altered in 1936–38. The porte-cochere at the main entrance was removed and a GWR roundel added to the façade. Hardwick's original Louis XVI-style interiors were stripped out or hidden by art deco detailing. After the Second World War the Great Western Royal became part of the state-owned BTH group until it was sold in 1983. It is now the Hilton London Paddington.

Foyer with art deco detailing, 2012. (Hilton Hotels & Resorts)

Great Northern Hotel, King's Cross, and the clock tower of St Pancras station, 2013. (Wayne Robson)

To solve the problem of a site with a curving boundary, the architect Lewis Cubitt designed the Great Northern Hotel as crescent-shaped. Opened in 1854, the Great Northern Railway's hotel had five storeys and an attic, something of a gamble in the days before lifts, when guests expected to pay less for rooms on upper floors. Guests in the sixty-nine-bedroom hotel did need to be wary of extra charges such as for coal fires and hot baths. In 1923 the hotel transferred to the LNER and, after nationalisation, became a British Transport Hotel. Sold in 1984, it is now a Tribute Portfolio Hotel with the ground floor converted into a shopping arcade.

The hotel in 2014. (Stephen Mason)

Grosvenor Hotel, Victoria, *c.* 1894. (James Lewis Collection)

Victoria station opened in 1860 as the West End terminus for both the London Brighton & South Coast and London Chatham & Dover railway companies. Adjoining the LBSCR station, the Grosvenor Hotel opened in 1861. Designed by J. T. Knowles, the façade of Bath stone and yellow brick is elaborately decorated. Some 150 feet in height and with 300 bedrooms, the building has a steep mansard roof with attics, dormers, a long row of chimneys and pavilions at each end. Inside, a grand staircase rises from the foyer to an arcaded gallery with classical columns and a panelled ceiling. The restaurant and lounge are also richly decorated.

Staircase with arcaded gallery above, 2014. (Marie-Annick Vigne)

Lounge, 2012. (Grosvenor Hotel)

The Grosvenor Victoria was one of the first hotels in London to be equipped with a lift, marking the beginning of the end for the practice of charging more for bedrooms on the lower floors. Previously independent, the hotel was purchased by the LBSCR in 1899. Along with major improvements to the station, a large extension to the hotel opened in 1907. This new section was nine storeys high, surmounted by pavilion roofs and outsize chimneys, contained 150 bedrooms and, in complete contrast with the original hotel, was in red brick and Portland stone with three giant pediments and a clock flanked by reclining female figures.

The 1907 extension (centre) with the original building on the right. (Oliver Mallich, 2009)

The hotel in 2006. (Grosvenor Hotel)

For much of its existence the Grosvenor Victoria was not railway owned. It was acquired by BTH in 1977. Stone cleaning in 1978 revealed its magnificent external decoration, previously hidden under a century of grime. It was sold back into the private sector in 1983 and is now part of the Guoman Hotels group.

Holborn Viaduct Hotel, *c.* 1900. (Wikimedia Commons*)

Holborn Viaduct station was opened in 1874 by the London Chatham & Dover Railway for domestic services and Continental boat trains. The station frontage was largely taken up by the Holborn Viaduct Hotel, opened in 1877. The hotel closed in 1917, after which it was used as offices. The building suffered severe bomb damage in 1941 and was demolished in 1963.

City Terminus Hotel, Cannon Street, 1867.

Opened by the South Eastern Railway in 1867, the City Terminus Hotel was designed by Edward Middleton Barry in Italianate style. Criticised for the cost of its lavish decoration, it specialised in catering for City functions and banquets held in its grand public rooms. The eighty-four bedrooms and five bathrooms were located on the upper floors, those at the back much affected by noise and smoke from the station. It was renamed the Cannon Street Hotel in 1879. The Southern Railway closed the hotel in 1931 and converted it to railway offices. The building suffered severe bomb damage in 1941 but was rebuilt. It was demolished in 1960.

Cannon Street Hotel. (Author's collection)

Midland Grand Hotel, St Pancras. (St Pancras Renaissance Hotel)

The Midland Railway was determined to make a splash with its new London terminus and hotel at St Pancras and commissioned leading architect Sir George Gilbert Scott to design the Midland Grand Hotel. The station opened in 1868 but the east wing of the hotel was not ready until 1873 and the remainder until 1876. The building is in an exuberant Gothic style in red brick, with stone dressings and polished granite columns. The façade includes a 90-degree curve at one end, a central tower modelled on the Cloth Hall at Ypres and a clock tower surmounted by a steeple. Gables, pinnacles and hooded dormers lend a fantasy quality to the roofline.

The original coffee lounge. (St Pancras Renaissance Hotel)

Gilbert Scott Restaurant, formerly the coffee lounge, 2015. (St Pancras Renaissance Hotel)

Inside, the lavish decoration included columns, friezes, chandeliers, marble fireplaces, mosaic tiling, carved stone arches and richly patterned wallpaper. A grand staircase mounted to a landing with vaulted ceiling. The sumptuous public rooms included a curved coffee lounge and a ladies' smoking room. Bedrooms numbered 300, some with private suites, and a glazed screen reduced smoke and noise from the station. Ownership passed to the LMS in 1923 but, by the mid 1930s, the Midland Grand was in need of modernisation and had become unprofitable, due in part to the unsustainable army of staff needed to keep it going. It closed in 1935.

Ladies' smoking room, 2014. (St Pancras Renaissance Hotel)

Grand staircase, 2011. (St Pancras Renaissance Hotel)

The building was used as railway offices until 1985, becoming increasingly run down. There was a threat of demolition but, in 1967, the building received Grade I listed status. British Rail arranged partial cleaning of the exterior in 1977–81, revealing its true glory from under a century of grime, a process completed in the 1990s. Work then started on the interior, exposing long-forgotten details. The building's final rehabilitation came in the form of a decision to use St Pancras as the terminus of the Channel Tunnel Rail Link. The hotel, restored to its former magnificence, reopened in 2011 as the St Pancras Renaissance Hotel, part of the Marriott group.

Not all hotel rooms look the same – the Sir George Gilbert Scott suite, 2011. (St Pancras Renaissance Hotel)

Great Eastern Hotel, Liverpool Street, 1980. (Author)

The Great Eastern Hotel provided the frontage of Liverpool Street station, with the rear of the hotel backing on to the buffer-stop end of the main line platforms. One set of tracks originally continued under the giant curved pediment of the hotel to allow supplies to be delivered. Opened in 1884, the Great Eastern Railway's hotel was designed by Charles Barry Jnr, while a 1901–3 extension was the work of Sir Robert Edis. In Dutch Renaissance style, the building's five storeys are in red brick with stone dressings. There are attic dormers and a tower at one corner, while the end facing Bishopsgate is topped by an elaborate stepped gable.

The giant curved pediment overlooking the station, 1982. (Author)

Hamilton Hall, now a public house, 2007. (Gürkan Sengün*)

The Great Eastern was primarily geared to catering for the needs of the city. The opulent public rooms looked to history for inspiration: for example, Louis XV rococo for the Hamilton Hall's ornate ceiling. There were two Masonic temples, one in Ancient Greek style with marble pillars, the other Ancient Egyptian. The hotel was absorbed by the LNER in 1923 and eventually became part of the nationalised BTH group. It was sold when BTH was broken up in 1983. Closed in 1996, the hotel reopened in 2000 following restoration. Now with 267 bedrooms, it has been renamed The Andaz Liverpool Street, a brand of the Hyatt Hotels group.

Masonic temple, 2011. (Richard Parmiter)

Great Central Hotel, Marylebone, *c.* 1910. (Philip Richards Collection)

The Great Central Hotel never operated as a hotel while in railway ownership, but the building played a key role in the post-war history of Britain's railways. It was built on land opposite the Great Central Railway's new London terminus at Marylebone, the two being linked by an ornate glass and iron porte-cochere. Because of financial difficulties, the hotel was sold brand new to Frederick Hotels Ltd, opening in 1899. Designed by Sir Robert Edis in French Renaissance style, it contained 700 bedrooms, a marble staircase, palm court and winter gardens. There was even a cycle track on the roof.

The original dining room. (The Landmark London)

The Landmark London, formerly Great Central Hotel. (The Landmark London)

With a prominent clock tower, the red-brick façade was decorated with elaborate terracotta detailing. The Great Central was requisitioned in the First World War as a military convalescent home and in the Second as an MI9 debriefing and interrogation centre. In 1945 the LNER bought the hotel to replace its own bomb-damaged offices. Later the building became the headquarters of British Railways, and was often referred to by staff as 'The Kremlin'. Sold off in the 1980s, the building has since been completely renovated to restore it to its original purpose and is now a 300-room luxury hotel, The Landmark London.

Porte-cochere linking hotel (left) and station entrance (right), 2015. (Peter Dean)

Big City Hotels

The first railway hotel in any of the big cities outside London opened in Birmingham in 1839. It was a makeshift affair and was eventually replaced by something more permanent. Most of the big city railway hotels were built between 1860 and 1890, but the early 1900s saw the opening of four of the grandest in Edinburgh, Manchester and Liverpool.

Birmingham Curzon Street station. (Tony Hisgett, 2009)

The London & Birmingham Railway opened in 1838 with termini at Euston and Curzon Street, both designed by Philip Hardwick. The need for a hotel at Birmingham quickly became apparent, and so in 1839 rooms in the station building were hastily converted to provide about ten bedrooms. Originally called the Victoria Hotel, a new wing was added in 1840 and it was renamed the Queens. It closed when a new station and hotel were opened at New Street in 1854 to cope with rapidly growing demand. Largely unused for many years, the original Grade I listed building still stands, awaiting a new role as the Birmingham terminus of the HS2 high-speed line.

Queens Hotel, Birmingham New Street, 1854.

Birmingham New Street station opened in 1854, with the new Queens Hotel incorporated into the station buildings. It was designed for the London & North Western Railway by William Livock in an Italianate style. In 1872 a threat to build a rival hotel called the North Western prompted the LNWR to rename the hotel the Queens & North Western. Originally with sixty bedrooms, it was extended several times until by 1925 there were 220 in total. In 1923 the Queens transferred to the new LMS. During the Second World War, part of the hotel served as an American Red Cross hostel.

Queens & North Western Hotel in LNWR days. (Author's collection)

Queens Hotel, 1927. (Frank Sweeney Collection)

During the hotel's lifetime, guests included Queen Victoria, George V and Queen Mary, General de Gaulle, Noel Coward and Mae West. After nationalisation the Queens began to attract criticism for its increasingly run-down state. Despite protests from the city and regular users, it was closed in 1965 and demolished by British Rail so that New Street station could be rebuilt as part of the West Coast Main Line electrification project.

Birmingham Snow Hill station and Great Western Hotel, c. 1905. (Author's collection)

The Great Western Railway opened a small hotel in part of Snow Hill station in 1863. Although the Great Western Hotel was praised by some guests, others complained about being kept awake at night by the rumble of passing freight trains. When redevelopment of the station began in 1906, the hotel was closed and converted for office use. Despite a campaign to save them, the station buildings were demolished in 1969.

Royal Victoria Hotel, Sheffield, 1982. (Author)

Built in 1862, the Victoria Hotel was bought by the Manchester Sheffield & Lincolnshire Railway in 1883 having already acquired the 'Royal' prefix following a visit by the Prince of Wales in 1875. The architect M. E. Hadfield designed a four-storey building in red brick with an ornate glass and iron canopy over the entrance. Inside, the public rooms are sumptuously decorated with panelled ceilings, pilasters and cornices. The Royal Victoria Hotel was taken over by the LNER in 1923 and later joined the state-owned BTH group. Sheffield Victoria station stood alongside the hotel but closed in 1970. Sold in 1982, the hotel is now a 107-bedroom Holiday Inn.

One of several oriental wall panels in the public rooms, 1982. (Author)

Central Station Hotel, Newcastle – the drawing room in NER days. (Author's collection)

John Dobson was the architect for both Newcastle Central station and its adjoining hotel. The magnificent station opened in 1850, the North Eastern Railway's more modest fifty-bedroom Central Station Hotel in 1854. Thomas Prosser redesigned and greatly extended the hotel in 1863, and the number of bedrooms was expanded to 133 in 1892 by the addition of two floors and a five-storey extension designed by William Bell.

Central Station Hotel, 1863. (Billy Embleton's collection)

This remarkable photograph shows the Central Station Hotel as it was over 150 years ago. The hotel is in the centre with the massive portico of Newcastle Central station projecting out towards the right in the background. On the left, the train sheds of the station can be seen. The hotel in this photograph now forms the right-hand section of the present hotel, to which two additional floors were added in 1892.

Royal Station Hotel, 2013. (Mike Quinn)

The entrance has an ornate glazed canopy, while the opulent interiors include a grand staircase and decorative tiling. In 1923 the LNER took over and in 1930 renamed it the Royal Station Hotel in recognition of earlier royal visits. After the Second World War it became a state-owned British Transport Hotel until 1983. It now operates as a Cairn Group hotel.

Lobby and staircase, 2010. (Royal Station Hotel, Newcastle)

Great Victoria Hotel, Bradford, 2013. (Nick Rowlands)

Designed by Yorkshire architects Lockwood & Mawson, the Victoria Hotel opened in 1867. French in style with Italianate touches, it stands four storeys high and is built principally of sandstone. Victorian census returns show that it attracted businessmen from all over the world visiting what was then an international centre for the woollen trade. Following the rebuilding of Bradford Exchange station opposite, the hotel was purchased by the Great Northern Railway in 1892 and renamed the Great Northern Victoria Hotel. In 1923 it became an LNER hotel. After nationalisation it was sold in 1952 and now operates under the name Great Victoria Hotel.

Midland Hotel, Bradford. (Robert Wade Collection)

Midland Hotel in 2015. (Tim Green)

Bradford's Midland Hotel opened in 1890 as part of a scheme to redevelop the adjacent Market Street station, later renamed Forster Square. Guests could use a tiled passageway linking the two. The ninety-bedroom hotel was designed by the Midland Railway's official architect, Charles Trubshaw, and its most prominent feature is a five-sided domed tower over the main entrance. The actor Sir Henry Irving died in the hotel in 1905. In 1923 it became an LMS hotel. After nationalisation it was a British Transport Hotel, but closed in 1975 and was sold. Reopened in 1993 and now restored to its former glory, the Midland is part of the Peel Hotels Group.

Tiled passageway linking hotel to station, 2014. (Kieran Wilkinson)

Former North Western Hotel, Liverpool, 2012. (Tony Hisgett)

Liverpool's first railway-built hotel was opened by the London & North Western Railway in 1871 at Lime Street station. The five-storey North Western Hotel was designed by Alfred Waterhouse in French Renaissance style, the roofline having a striking array of dormers, chimneys, towers and spires. With 200 bedrooms but only eight bathrooms and thirty-seven toilets, the LMS decided to close the hotel in 1933 rather than meet the high cost of modernisation. The building was used as offices until 1970 but then lay empty until 1994 when it was bought by Liverpool John Moores University, which converted it into a student hall of residence.

Aerial view of Lime Street station and the former North Western Hotel, 2012. (Sean Gibson)

Former Exchange Station Hotel, Liverpool. (Alan Maycock, 2010)

Liverpool's Exchange Hotel was opened by the Lancashire & Yorkshire Railway in 1888 next to the company's Exchange station. Designed by Henry Shelmerdine, its eighty bedrooms were separated from the noise and smoke by a carriage concourse. A decorative iron entrance canopy stretched out over the pavement. The kitchens were located on the top floor, making it difficult to keep food fresh in summer. Ownership transferred to the LMS in 1923 and, after nationalisation, it became part of the BTH group. The hotel closed in 1971 and was used as offices before demolition of the interior, leaving only the façade to screen a new office development.

Ornamental iron canopy at the hotel entrance, 2010. (Alan Maycock)

Adelphi Hotel, Liverpool, *c.* 1914. (Author's collection)

By the late nineteenth century, Liverpool had established itself as Britain's pre-eminent transatlantic port. Following the success of the city's two other railway hotels, the Midland Railway, operating from Central Station, bought the Adelphi Hotel in 1892, but it quickly proved too small. The company decided to build a new Adelphi as 'a building worthy of a great commercial city like Liverpool'. Using modern building techniques, the white Portland stone façade was constructed around a steel skeleton. Designed by Frank Atkinson, architect of Selfridges store in London, the Midland Adelphi opened in 1914 with nearly 600 rooms.

The hotel in 2009. (Andy Hebden)

Adelphi – the Central Court, 2012. (Martin H. Watson)

Facilities included two ballrooms, a swimming pool and Turkish baths. In contrast to the modern style of the exterior, the interior of the Adelphi was a riot of architectural styles: Ionic columns in the Hypostyle Hall, a restaurant in Louis XIV style, a Central Court resembling the lounge of an ocean liner, and decorative details anticipating the art deco style of the inter-war period. Innovations in the bedrooms included fixed wash basins with hot and cold taps instead of china bowls and jugs, built-in wardrobes, and wooden beds rather than traditional brass bedsteads. Despite the installation of central heating, fireplaces were provided in every room.

Hypostyle Hall, 2012. (Martin H. Watson)

The Adelphi's Louis XIV-style restaurant, 2013. (Lawrence Martin)

The French restaurant was noted for its menu, although the ten-course inaugural banquet in March 1914 must have left those present groaning. Guests at the hotel have included US President Franklin D. Roosevelt, Winston Churchill, Frank Sinatra and Judy Garland. The Adelphi passed into the ownership of the LMS in 1923. After the Second World War it became part of the state-owned BTH group. It was sold in 1983 and, renamed the Britannia Adelphi, is now part of the Britannia Hotels group.

Bedroom, 2011. (Chemical Engineer*)

North British Hotel, Glasgow, *c.* 1900. (Frank Sweeney Collection)

In 1877 the North British Railway rebuilt its Glasgow terminus at Queen Street and at about the same time purchased the adjoining Queens Hotel, which dates from the 1780s, renaming it the North British. The handsome Georgian façade looks out over George Square. The company later rebuilt the hotel, adding a third floor. In 1923 the NBR and its hotel were absorbed by the LNER and, after railway nationalisation, the North British became a British Transport Hotel. Sold in 1984, it was renamed the Diplomat. It is now the Millennium Hotel, owned by the hotel chain of that name.

The hotel in 1981. (Author)

St Enoch Hotel, Glasgow, 1890s. (Library of Congress*)

The Glasgow & South Western Railway's St Enoch Hotel opened in 1879. Designed by Thomas Wilson and built on a grand scale, the towering dark red sandstone structure contained 200 bedrooms. The music hall artiste Florrie Forde was a regular guest and is said to have kept her pet parrot at the porter's lodge while she went on stage. In 1923 ownership passed to the LMS. During the Second World War much of the hotel was taken over by the Royal Navy as HMS *Spartiate*. It later joined the state-owned BTH group but closed in 1974. Part of the entrance hall's mosaic floor depicting the GSWR's coat-of-arms was saved during demolition in 1977.

Preserved section of mosaic floor from the entrance hall, 2009. (James Carson)

Central Station Hotel, Glasgow, in LMS days. (Frank Sweeney Collection)

Originally intended as an office block, the Caledonian Railway's Central Station Hotel opened in 1885. The architect Robert Rowand Anderson designed a vast 400-room, L-shaped building in sandstone, flanking two sides of the station. The main entrance with its decorative glass-and-iron porch is on a street corner where the two wings meet. Standing alongside is an impressive square clock tower topped by a cupola. The station is noted for its collection of curving, dark-stained wooden buildings, among them the hotel's domed circular lounge – now the Champagne Bar – located at first floor level above passenger facilities on the concourse.

The domed circular hotel lounge seen from the station concourse, 1979. (Author)

Grand Central Hotel, 2015. (Marshall Smart)

The public rooms had electric lighting from the start and this was available throughout the hotel by 1890. Coal for the boilers was delivered by rail hopper wagons, which emptied their contents down a chute into the basement. When customers complained about the quality of the whisky in 1896, it emerged that some skulduggery had been going on somewhere in the supply chain; the hotel had to make amends rapidly by buying in some top quality malts. Several extensions to cope with demand meant that by 1921 the Central Hotel could accommodate 550 guests, who had to navigate corridors up to 343 feet long to reach their rooms.

Champagne bar, 2014. (Kay Williams)

Central Hotel – entrance to the Malmaison restaurant, 1979. (Author)

In 1923 the Central Hotel transferred to the LMS and in 1948 became state-owned and eventually a British Transport Hotel. Attached to the hotel was one of Glasgow's most exclusive and expensive restaurants – the Malmaison – accessible from the street under a glass canopy in the shape of a scalloped shell. In 1979 the stonework around the hotel's main entrance was cleaned. The result was so striking that the rest of the façade was similarly treated in the 1980s, revealing the natural colour of the sandstone. The hotel was sold in 1983. It has since been renamed the Grand Central and is part of the PH Hotels group. It is a Category A listed building.

Stone-cleaned main entrance, 1979. (Author)

Caledonian Hotel, Edinburgh, *c.* 1920. (Frank Sweeney Collection)

The Caledonian Railway had long planned a hotel for its Princes Street terminus in Edinburgh but lack of funds prevented progress. The ground-floor station buildings were completed years before work on the Princes Street Station Hotel began in 1899. The V-shaped site led the architects Peddie & Browne to design a triangular building with the sharp end cut off to provide the hotel's main entrance. The façade is in distinctive pink sandstone with a giant Dutch gable above the entrance. The foyer was in marble and a grand T-shaped staircase was lit by stained glass displaying the coats-of-arms of towns served by the railway.

Waldorf Astoria – The Caledonian, 2012. (Adam Smith)

The Caledonian seen from Edinburgh Castle, 2009. (David McNeish)

The 205-room hotel opened in 1903. The name Princes Street Station Hotel was soon changed to Caledonian Station Hotel and finally to the Caledonian Hotel. In 1923 the hotel was absorbed by the new LMS, and after nationalisation eventually became a British Transport Hotel. Princes Street station was closed in 1965 and subsequently demolished, allowing the hotel to expand; a notable feature is the Peacock Alley bar and lounge area, which was created by roofing over the old station concourse and ticket hall. The Caledonian was sold in 1981. It now operates under Hilton Hotels' Waldorf Astoria branding. The building is listed Category A.

'Peacock Alley' – formerly Princes Street station concourse, now part of the hotel, 2014. (Waldorf Astoria Hotels & Resorts)

North British Station Hotel, Edinburgh, and Princes Street Gardens, 1914. (Mike Ashworth Collection)

Construction of the North British Station Hotel began in 1895. The ten-storey building rises from platform level at Edinburgh Waverley station with only the top six storeys visible above Princes Street on which the main entrance is located. A clock tower, rising 190 feet above street level, houses the hotel's water tanks and dominates the façade. The clock is traditionally set three minutes fast with the aim of ensuring that passengers do not miss their trains. Designed for the North British Railway by William Hamilton Beattie, the architecture is a combination of Scottish Baronial and Continental styles with a heavy Edwardian accent.

The soot-blackened North British in 1958. (Allan Hailstone)

Balmoral Hotel, formerly the North British, and Edinburgh Waverley station, 2012. (Malcolm Cowe)

In sandstone reinforced with 1,600 tons of steel, the North British Station Hotel was built around a central well which was roofed at street level, forming a domed palm court beneath. When the hotel opened in 1902, a special blend of whisky named 'NB' was manufactured in the basements. The 700 rooms included more than 300 bedrooms, seventy lavatories and fifty-two bathrooms. A number of suites were provided for permanent residents. Outward-facing rooms were double-glazed to reduce noise and offered views of Edinburgh.

Palm court, 2014. (Balmoral Hotel)

Balmoral Hotel, 2012. (Paul Murray)

The public rooms were opulent. Guests were greeted by an imposing entrance hall and reception area. The long dining room occupied the frontage at street level, giving a view of the castle. Central heating, air conditioning and electric lifts were provided. Staff and guests' servants were accommodated in the attics. In the 1920s the hotel became part of the LNER and had its name shortened to the North British. After railway nationalisation the hotel eventually joined the BTH group and was sold in 1981. After closing for refurbishment, it reopened in 1991 as the Balmoral and is now a Rocco Forte hotel.

Lobby, 2014. (Balmoral Hotel)

Midland Hotel, Manchester, early 1900s. (Author's collection)

The vast, imposing Midland Hotel was designed by the Midland Railway's official architect, Charles Trubshaw. The highly ornamented red-brick exterior with brown terracotta detailing was built around a steel frame in a style sometimes referred to as Edwardian Baroque. Manchester Central station opposite was linked to the hotel by a glazed covered way. William Towle, the Midland Railway's hotels manager, was determined that the Midland would be the last word in luxury when it opened in 1903. It had four restaurants, a banqueting hall, winter garden, Turkish baths and an 800-seat theatre with its own repertory company.

'The Beautiful Hall' – the 800-seat theatre, *c.* 1905. (Frank Sweeney Collection)

Midland Hotel, Manchester, 2011. (Daniel Fernandez)

On fine days afternoon tea could be taken on the roof terrace, accompanied by an orchestra. It was at the Midland Hotel that Charles Rolls and Henry Royce first met in 1904. Of the hotel's 500 bedrooms, those facing the street were double-glazed to reduce noise and a number of suites were provided to cater for permanent residents. The theatre closed in 1922 and the space was converted into three floors of bedrooms. The LMS took over the hotel in 1923. During the Second World War, the hotel escaped serious damage; it was said that Hitler wanted the hotel to become Gestapo headquarters if his plans to invade Britain had succeeded.

Main entrance with the golden wyvern, symbol of the Midland Railway, 2008. (Mike Smith)

Afternoon tea in the Midland Hotel's French Room, 2012. (Michael J. Savage)

After the war, the Midland became part of the state-owned BTH group. Manchester Central station closed in 1969 and has since been converted into the Manchester Central Convention Complex – an exhibition, sporting and conference venue – providing the hotel with a new source of custom. Restored and modernised, the Manchester Midland now forms part of the Q Hotels group. The building is listed Grade II*.

A link with the past. (Karen Thompson)

This 2008 photograph shows the backstairs ash chute in the Midland Hotel still bearing a faded instruction by Arthur Towle, Controller of LMS Hotels from 1925 to 1944. Arthur was the son of Sir William Towle, the Midland Railway's hotels supremo who oversaw construction of the hotel.

The first Queens Hotel, Leeds (extreme right), *c.* 1908. (Author's collection)

The Midland Railway's first hotel in Leeds opened in 1863, partly to give passengers using the company's new Anglo-Scottish route a midway point to break their journey. It was such a success that the Queens Hotel was extended twice. An LMS hotel from 1923, it closed in 1935 to be completely rebuilt in 1936/7 along with Leeds City station. The rebuild was designed by W. Curtis Green, architect of London's Dorchester Hotel, and William Hamlyn, the LMS's architect, using steel-frame construction techniques. Clad in white Portland stone with evenly spaced windows on seven floors, the notably plain façade combines classical Greek with art deco.

The new Queens Hotel, late 1930s. (Author's collection)

Queens Hotel, 2010. (Tom Bastin)

All 206 bedrooms were provided with telephones, bathrooms, air conditioning and central heating rather than coal fires. There were six passenger lifts and eight more for goods and staff. Emphasis was placed on reducing noise inside and outside the hotel through features such as double-glazing, sound-resistant floors and rubber paving bricks on the station approach. Even the tram lines were moved 30 feet further away. In contrast with the plain façade, the interior was colourful and had art deco detailing, some of which remains. After nationalisation, the Queens eventually became a BTH hotel. Sold in 1984, it is now part of the Q Hotels group.

Art deco corridor, 2010. (George Clixby)

Leisure Hotels

The ever-expanding railway network fuelled the growth of tourism and seaside holidays in the late nineteenth century. Railway hotels began to appear at resorts and tourist destinations in the 1860s. Some offered sporting activities but hotels principally dedicated to golfers were mostly built during the early years of the twentieth century. Between the wars a few grand country houses were converted into railway hotels.

Keswick Hotel, Keswick, Cumbria, 2004. (Michael Duffy)

The railway came to Keswick in the form of the Cockermouth, Keswick & Penrith Railway. Passenger services began in 1865 and, in 1869, the company built the four-storey Keswick Hotel alongside the station with a view to catering for visitors to the Lake District. An enclosed passageway linked the station and hotel. The hotel was sold off just before the 1923 grouping of railway companies. After the railway closed in 1972, the hotel bought the main station building and converted it to provide additional bedrooms and a section of the station's canopy was glassed in to form a lounge.

Zetland Hotel, Saltburn-by-the-Sea, Yorkshire, in NER days. (Author's collection)

In 1861 the Stockton & Darlington Railway was extended to Saltburn to exploit its potential as a seaside resort. A special platform served the company's new thirty-seven-bedroom Zetland Hotel, which opened in 1863 – the same year the North Eastern Railway absorbed the S&DR. Designed in Italianate style by William Peachey, the hotel catered principally for holidaymakers. A telescope room at the top of its semi-circular tower offered panoramic views. In 1923 ownership passed to the LNER. After the Second World War the Zetland became a BTH hotel but later struggled to attract business. It was sold in 1975, closed in 1983 and was converted into flats in 1989.

The former hotel in 2007. (Andrew Clayton)

Tregenna Castle Hotel, St Ives, Cornwall, 2013. (Philip Vayro)

Built as a private house in 1774, the two-storey granite mansion is notable for its castellations and corner towers. GWR leased the building in 1878 following the opening of the branch line to St Ives and converted it into the Tregenna Castle Hotel, with tennis courts, a putting green and nine-hole golf course. The GWR purchased it outright in 1895. Joachim von Ribbentrop, Hitler's ambassador to Britain in the 1930s, took his family on holiday to the hotel and enjoyed it so much that he planned to make it his home if Germany won the war. Instead it was nationalised in 1948 and remained a BTH hotel until its sale in 1983. It remains open.

The hotel seen from the gardens, 2015. (Robert Schaub)

Hotel Imperial, Hythe, Kent, 2005. (Hythe Imperial)

The South Eastern Railway opened the hotel in 1880 as the Seabrook. It was renamed Hotel Imperial about 1900. Guests enjoyed the use of tennis courts, a putting green and golf course, as well as sea bathing from the adjacent beach. In 1923 the hotel transferred to the new Southern Railway. It was sold in 1946 following war service. Greatly enlarged, it now operates as the Hythe Imperial, a Classic British Hotel.

North Western Hotel, Blaenau Ffestiniog, Wales, 1962. (Ron Fisher)

In 1881 the London & North Western Railway built the North Western Hotel to encourage visitors to explore the Conway Valley and Snowdonia. Patronage did not meet expectations and the hotel was sold in 1906. It then served as a public house before eventual demolition. This 1962 photograph shows the hotel on the left, with the tracks of the narrow-gauge Ffestiniog Railway still awaiting restoration and reopening.

Station hotel, Ayr, Scotland, 1890s. (Library of Congress*)

The Glasgow & South Western Railway opened the station hotel at the coastal resort of Ayr in 1886. Four storeys with pavilions at each end and a prominent corner tower near the centre, the red sandstone building dominates the station and contains its main entrance and offices. The hotel's main purpose was to cater for holidaymakers from Glasgow and the west of Scotland. The LMS took over in 1923 but patronage declined. The hotel was sold in 1951 after nationalisation but remained open for many years. Currently closed, there is some uncertainty about its future. The building has been placed on the Buildings at Risk Register for Scotland.

Ayr station and station hotel, 1986. (Gordon Edgar)

Cruden Bay Hotel, Aberdeenshire, Scotland. (Erroll Schoolhouse collection)

The Cruden Bay Hotel on the Aberdeenshire coast was specially designed to cater for golfers. As there was no railway within 10 miles, the Great North of Scotland Railway built a branch line to bring guests to its ninety-six-bedroom hotel and golf course, and an electric tramway to connect the hotel to the new station. Opened in 1899, the spectacular granite hotel at first attracted an affluent clientele but its fortunes gradually declined. The LNER took over in 1923 but closed the railway in 1932, the tramway in 1940 and the hotel itself after war service as a military hospital. The building was sold in 1951 and demolished the following year.

Cruden Bay Hotel tram No. 1. (Author's Collection)

Station hotel, Turnberry, Ayrshire, Scotland, *c.* 1908. (Frank Sweeney Collection)

In 1906 the Glasgow & South Western opened a light railway between Girvan and Ayr to serve communities on the Ayrshire coast. One stop was at Turnberry, where the G&SWR had built a seventy-eight-bedroom hotel and two golf courses. On a bluff overlooking the Firth of Clyde, Turnberry's station hotel offered guests salt water plunge baths and special facilities for golfers. Designed by James Miller, the hotel's long façade is in white-rendered brick, broken by gables and loggias, with a steep red-tiled roof with attic dormers. Although most guests arrived by train, the rise of the car meant that special accommodation had to be provided for chauffeurs.

Lobby and tea lounge in LMS days. (Turnberry Hotel)

Turnberry Hotel, 2012. (Antonina Mitchell)

With fixtures and fittings of the highest quality, the hotel was far too grand to be called the station hotel for long and was quickly renamed the Turnberry. During the First World War the hotel was requisitioned for use as a military hospital and the golf courses were flattened to provide a training base for the new Royal Flying Corps. The hotel and courses were restored under the ownership of the LMS but in the Second World War it was again used as a military hospital and airbase. After the war it became a state-owned BTH hotel until sold in 1983. The hotel is now owned by the American tycoon Donald Trump and has been restyled Trump Turnberry.

Hotel façade, 2011. (Gordon Cunningham)

Dornoch Hotel, Scottish Highlands, 2012. (Stephen Gallagher)

Opened by the Highland Railway in 1904, the eighty-three-bedroom Dornoch Hotel adjoins the Royal Dornoch golf course. It was originally served by a light railway connecting into the Inverness–Wick line. The LMS took ownership in 1923. Prompted by declining patronage, British Transport Hotels sold the Dornoch in 1965. Now part of the Bay Hotels group, it remains an attractive base for golfers and walkers.

Highland Hotel, Strathpeffer, Scotland, 1980. (Alan Longmuir)

The Highland Railway opened the ninety-bedroom Highland Hotel in 1911, its half-timbered gables, attic dormers and corner towers dominating the town. In 1923 it was absorbed by the LMS. When the branch line to Strathpeffer closed in 1946 it was decided to sell the hotel, although British Transport Hotels completed the sale only in 1958. The hotel remains open as part of the Bay Hotels group.

The former Felix Hotel, Felixstowe, Suffolk, 2015. (John Bugg)

First opened in 1903, the grand and elegant 199-bedroom Felix Hotel was purchased by the Great Eastern Railway in 1920. Standing close to the beach in 16 acres of grounds, the hotel had tennis courts, croquet lawns and a golf course. In 1923 ownership transferred to the LNER. The hotel was sold in 1952 for use as offices and has since been converted into retirement apartments.

Deepdene Hotel, Dorking, Surrey, *c.* 1920s. (Terence O'Brien Collection)

This former country house was turned into the ninety-room Deepdene Hotel and was bought by the Southern Railway about 1925. After the hotel closed in 1936 the building and tunnels in the grounds became the wartime headquarters of the Southern Railway, from where the transport of 320,000 allied troops evacuated from Dunkirk in May–June 1940 was controlled. This historic building was demolished in 1967.

Gleneagles Hotel, Perthshire, Scotland, 1920s. (Author's collection)

The Caledonian Railway's hotel at Gleneagles was eleven years in the making. Delayed by the First World War, it opened in 1924, by which time the company and its great 114-bedroom hotel designed by Matthew Adam had been absorbed into the new LMS. The moorland in the immediate vicinity was transformed into two superb golf courses and Gleneagles quickly became world famous as a golfing hotel. In addition, there were tennis courts, an indoor swimming pool, bowling greens, croquet lawns, and facilities for angling and grouse shooting, giving Gleneagles the reputation of Britain's premier sports hotel.

The hotel in BTH days. (Gleneagles Hotel)

Gleneagles in 2010. (Donald Thornton)

The ballroom could accommodate 200 couples, and the hotel's opening was celebrated with a concert of dance music led by bandleader Henry Hall, which was relayed live in one of the earliest BBC outside broadcasts. An LMS employee for eight years, Hall founded orchestras in most LMS hotels before becoming leader of the BBC dance orchestra. Gleneagles was requisitioned during the Second World War, which caused a financial problem as it received far less per annum for war service compared with its pre-war profits. After the war, Gleneagles was nationalised and eventually became part of the BTH group.

The garden front, 2008. (Justin Goring)

Gleneagles kitchen brigade in BTH days, head chef Robert Cottet front centre. (Gleneagles Hotel)

By 1969 the number of bedrooms had increased to 210 and Gleneagles won plaudits from renowned critic Egon Ronay for its cuisine under head chef Robert Cottet. BTH sold the hotel in 1981, and since then the hotel has retained its unique reputation as a sporting and conference centre. In 2005 it hosted the G8 summit of world leaders and in 2014 the Ryder Cup.

Old Course Hotel, St. Andrews, Scotland, 2015. (Mike Smith)

The Old Course was the only new hotel built by the BTH group and can therefore claim to be the last of Britain's railway hotels. Built in 1968 and designed by Curtis & Davis, the hotel overlooks the world famous golf course at St. Andrews. The hotel was sold in 1982 and has been greatly extended by its new owners.

Welcombe Hotel, Stratford-upon-Avon, Warwickshire, 2010. (Richard Croft)

Welcombe House was a private residence designed by Henry Clutton in the 1860s for a Manchester cotton magnate. With Tudor and Jacobean features, the house overlooks a terraced garden with fine views over the surrounding countryside. Interior features include a great hall. The LMS bought the house in 1930 for conversion into the 131-bedroom Welcombe Hotel. It opened in 1931 with a new wing added in 1933. Guests could enjoy tennis, fishing and boating. After railway nationalisation the Welcombe eventually became part of the BTH group. Sold in 1983, it is now styled Hallmark Hotel The Welcombe. The building is listed Grade II*.

The Great Hall, 2010. (Richard Croft)

Bovey Castle, formerly the Manor House Hotel, Moretonhampstead, Devon, 2013.
(Tony Kerr)

North Bovey Manor was built in 1907 as a family residence for Viscount Hambledon
(W. H. Smith). Detmar Blow, a leading architect of large country houses, designed a
Jacobean-style manor house with a long irregular façade. Built of granite, the house is set
on a balustraded terrace. Interior features include a panelled great hall and an Adam-style
drawing room. During the First World War, the house was used as a convalescent home
for officers. When the estate was sold to pay death duties in 1929, the GWR purchased
the house and 200 acres for conversion into the Manor House Hotel.

The terrace frontage, 2013. (Simon Wilkinson)

Cathedral Room, originally the Great Hall, 2015. (Bovey Castle)

New bathrooms and furniture were installed and an eighteen-hole golf course and tennis courts provided. The Manor House Hotel opened in 1930. In 1935 Blow designed an extension, which increased the number of rooms to sixty-six. Set on the edge of Dartmoor, the hotel was the filming location of the 1939 movie *The Hound of the Baskervilles* starring Basil Rathbone. During the Second World War the building was a military hospital. After the war it became a state-owned British Transport Hotel until it was sold in 1983. Renamed Bovey Castle in 2003, it is now part of the Eden Hotel Collection. The building is listed Grade II*.

Adam Room, 2015. (Bovey Castle)

The new Midland Hotel, Morecambe, Lancashire. (Author's collection)

In 1932 the LMS decided to replace its Victorian hotel in Morecambe with a modern forty-bedroom establishment on a curving promenade site opposite the station. Designed by Oliver Hill with murals and sculptures by Eric Gill, the new Midland Hotel opened in 1933. The long curving white frontage, central circular tower, concrete balconies, flat roof and circular tea room make it one of the classic art deco buildings of the 1930s. Yet, in the curves of one of the last railway hotels ever built there is just a faint echo of one of the first, Decimus Burton's semi circular North Euston Hotel at nearby Fleetwood.

Façade and Rotunda Bar (former tea room), 2009. (The Midland Morecambe)

Midland Hotel at dusk, 2015. (Keith Sergeant)

The new Midland enjoyed only six years as a hotel before being requisitioned for war service by the Royal Air Force. From 1939 until 1947 it was used as a military hospital. Changing post-war demand for seaside holidays led to its sale by the newly nationalised railway in 1952. The hotel continued to operate until 1993 after which, empty and neglected for a decade, its condition deteriorated until it was acquired by Urban Splash, a property company. In 2008 the Midland Hotel reopened, restored to its former glory and operated by English Lakes Hotels. It is a Grade II* listed building.

Looking up the central stairwell to Eric Gill's Neptune and Triton ceiling medallion, 2014. (Phil Beard)

Acknowledgements

I would like to thank the following people for permission to use their copyrighted photographs in this book: Tom Bastin, Phil Beard, J. L. Berghout, Mark Bissett, Mike Brocklebank, Ben Brooksbank, John Bugg, James Carson, Andrew Clayton, George Clixby, Malcolm Cowe, Mike Craig, Richard Croft, Gordon Cunningham, Peter Dean, Michael Duffy, Gordon Edgar, Brian Evans, Simon Evans, 'Failing_Angel', Daniel Fernandez, Ron Fisher, Stephen Gallagher, Sean Gibson, Justin Goring, Tim Green, Jack Guilliams, Alan Hailstone, Andy Hebden, Tony Hisgett, Tim Jenkinson, Peter Koppers, Hugh Llewelyn, Keith Long, Alan Longmuir, Fiona MacKintosh, Oliver Mallich, Lawrence Martin, Stephen Mason, Alan Maycock, Antonina Mitchell, Paul Murray, David McNeish, Alistair Parker, Richard Parmiter, Steve Poole, Mike Quinn, Malcolm Rhead, Wayne Robson, Nick Rowlands, Michael J. Savage, Robert Schaub, Keith Sergeant, Bernard Sharp, Marshall Smartt, Adam Smith, Mike Smith, Ian Taylor, Karen Thompson, Elizabeth Thomsen, Donald Thornton, Philip Vayro, Marie-Annick Vigne, Martin H. Watson, Mark Wheaver, Kieran Wilkinson, Simon Wilkinson, Gareth Williams, Kay Williams and David Wright.

I am also grateful to the following individuals and archives for allowing me to use images from their collections: Mike Ashworth, Gavin Bleakley, Billy Embleton, Erroll Schoolhouse, 'Harwich & Dovercourt', John Law, James Lewis, Medway City Archive, Dr Terence O'Brien, Philip Richards, Royan, 'Our Newhaven', Frank Sweeney and Robert Wade.

I have used some images under the terms of Creative Commons licences. These are denoted by an asterisk (*) next to the name of the photographer or image owner, namely 'Chemical Engineer', the Library of Congress and Gürkan Sengün.

I also record my thanks for the help given by representatives of the following hotels who have supplied photographs: Amba Hotel Charing Cross, Balmoral Hotel Edinburgh, Bovey Castle, Gleneagles, Grosvenor Hotel Victoria, Hilton London Paddington, Hythe Imperial, Mercure Hull Royal Hotel, Royal Station Hotel Newcastle, St Pancras Renaissance Hotel, The Landmark London, The Midland Morecambe, Trump Turnberry and Waldorf Astoria Edinburgh.

All images in this book remain the copyright of their photographer or owner.

The facts and figures in this book have been drawn from numerous sources. I would like to acknowledge in particular Oliver Carter's *An Illustrated History of British Railway Hotels 1838–1983* (Silver Link Publishing, 1990) and Gordon Biddle's *Britain's Historic Railway Buildings* (Ian Allen, 2011).

Every attempt has been made to seek permission for copyrighted material used in this book. However, if we have inadvertently used copyrighted material without permission or acknowledgement we apologise and we will make the necessary correction at the first opportunity.